Star Trash

by David Walke

Characters:

Captain Birk	Hoova
Mr Spick	Luke Skyscraper
Sweepy 3-0	Dustpan Solo
U-Bend	Flush Gordon
Princess Loofa	Muck Rogers
Lord Dark Vaper	Guard
Yabba the Shed	Spot
Narrator	Sound Effects - FX

Scene 1: *The Bin Ship*

Narr   Space - the final dump.
This is the story of the Bin-ship Boobyprise. Its job is to boldly go where no man has bin before.

Capt   Captain's log number 2-3-5-7-9-4-3-1-8-2.

Spick   Captain!

Capt   8-6-1-3-9-

Spick   Captain Birk!

Capt   Shut up, Spick! I'm doing the log. 5-1-3-6-

Spick   I've got a bleep on my screen.

Capt   You've got smelly feet as well.

2

Spick   It's a ship coming this way.

3-0   It's coming fast, sir.

Capt   Shut up, you two. I've made a mess of the log.

3-0   It's sending out a call for help.

Spick   The ship is calling for help, Captain. Someone on it needs help!

Capt   Tell them to get lost! I'll have to start again. 2-3-5-7-9-4…

3-0   It's a girl.

Capt   What?

Spick   There's someone calling for help, sir. It's a girl.

Capt   A girl? I remember them… I think…

Spick   I think you've been in space too long, Captain!

3-0   The ship is on the screen now, sir.

Spick   Yes, I can see it. I can see the ship. It's an… Oh, no!

Capt   What's an oh-no? What sort of a space-ship is an oh-no?

Spick	It's not a ship, Captain. It's a trash-bin.
Capt	We've found a girl out here in space. She's stuck in a trash-bin?
Prin	Hello! Is that a star-ship? Can you hear me?
Capt	This is the Bin-ship Boobyprise. Hello there! I'm Captain Birk. How can we help you?
Prin	Look, Birk, cut the chat. Beam me on to your ship!
3-0	I'll beam her on to the ship now, sir.
FX	ZONK ZONK.
Prin	Get back!
U-B	Meep meep.
Capt	There's two of them.
Spick	Yes, sir. There's a girl and a robot.
Capt	Which one is the girl?
Spick	You really have been in space too long, Captain.
3-0	The one that looks like a big tin can is the robot.

Spick   The one with the gun is the girl.

Capt   A gun! Hit the deck! Red alert!

FX   WOOP-WOOP-WOOP-WOOP.

Prin   Stop it! Stay back or I shoot!

Spick   Put the gun down, miss!

Prin   No! I need to check you out.

Capt   Don't shoot! Don't shoot!

Prin   The Umpire is after me! Do you work for the evil Umpire?

Spick   No, this is a bin-ship. We work for the Council.

Capt   Help! Help! Don't shoot me! I'm too young to die!

Spick   Put the gun down, miss.

Prin   Can I trust you?

3-0   You are safe with us. Put the gun down.

Prin   OK. The gun is down.

Capt   Don't shoot! Don't shoot! Help! Call the cops!

Spick   Captain! It's OK! The girl has put her gun down.

Capt   Oh, good. It's all over. I'm glad I sorted that out.

Prin   Are you nuts?

Capt   No, I'm Birk. I'm Captain Birk.

Prin   I'm Princess Loofa.

Capt   What! You are the Princess Loofa?

Spick   The Princess of the Council of Planets?

Prin   Yes, and this is my robot friend, U-Bend.

U-B   Meep meep.

Spick   What did he say?

3-0   He said 'meep meep'.

Capt   What does he mean? What does 'meep meep' mean?

Prin   He always says 'meep meep'.

Capt   He said it again. He said 'meep meep' again!

Prin   OK! OK! What's the big deal? I like him! I don't care if he says 'meep meep' or 'moop moop', or 'mip mip'. He's good for a pet and he doesn't eat much. So leave him alone.

Spick   Why are you in space in a trash-bin?

Prin   I had to escape! It was the only way. I hid in the trash-bin and blasted into space.

3-0   Captain, sir, I have a bleep on the screen.

Spick   It's a gun-ship, Captain. It's coming in fast!

Prin   Vaper!

Capt   Pardon?

Prin   It's the evil Dark Vaper! He's followed me!

Spick   Dark Vaper commands the Umpire's Death fleet.

Prin   Dark Vaper wants me. He's after me. We've got to fight!

Capt   You want to fight? But that hurts! Help! Help!

Spick   Turn the ship round, Sweepy. Let's get out of here.

Prin   You can't run from Dark Vaper. You've got to fight. Put your shields up.

Capt   We can't fight.

3-0   We haven't got any shields.

Prin   What do you do when you're under attack?

Capt   We just hang Spick's socks out of the window. That always seems to put them off.

Spick   He's coming in fast, Captain!

Prin   We've got to fight.

Capt   Oh, no! Help! Red alert! Red alert!

FX   WOOP-WOOP-WOOP-WOOP

3-0   It's going to be one of those days.

U-B   Meep meep.

Scene 2: *Dark Vaper*

Narr   The Boobyprise hung in space. Vaper's ship came up on it slowly. The gun-ship cast a shadow - black and evil.

Capt   Boo! Hiss! Down with Vaper!

3-0   Can we run for it, Captain?

Dark   Stop! Do not move. I am the Lord Dark Vaper!

Capt   Oh! Hi Dark, nice to see you. We just stopped for a cup of tea. So we'll be off now.

Dark   I command the Umpire's Death Fleet. Stop, or I will destroy you!

Capt   Thanks, Dark, and the same to you. Have a nice day.

Dark   I am looking for someone.

Capt   Well she's not here, Dark. I haven't got her. There's no Princess on my ship.

Dark   I did not say she was a Princess. You did. So she must be on your ship!

3-0   Whoops, it's show time.

U-B   Meep meep.

Dark   Stay back. I will beam on to your ship.

Prin   We've got to fight. Get your guns!

Spick   We have no guns, Princess. This is a bin-ship.

Prin   What do you do if there's an attack?

Capt   Like I said, we hang Spick's socks out of the window. If that doesn't work then Spick wiggles his ears at them. That always seems to give them a fright.

Prin   But you must have something. What do you fight with?

Capt   We've got some air-fresheners. They can bring you out in a nasty rash.

3-0   Here comes Dark Vaper.

Spick   He's got troops with him, Captain.

Prin   Get my gun, U-Bend. I'll stop Vaper!

U-B   Meep meep.

Dark   Stand back. I'm beaming over.

FX	ZONK ZONK ZONK ZONK.
Capt	Welcome aboard. This is your Captain. Your hostess today is the lovely Princess Loofa.
Prin	Eat star-dust, Vaper!
FX	ZAP ZAP ZAP.
Dark	Fire! Get them! I want the Princess alive!
FX	POW POW POW.
Capt	You won't get me, you smelly thing!
Spick	Air-fresheners ready! Scoot!
FX	PSHH PSHH PSHH.
Prin	Oh, no, U-Bend, my gun's empty!
U-B	Meep meep.
FX	POW POW POW... PSHH PSHH.
3-0	These air-fresheners are no good, Captain.
Spick	They won't stop Vaper.
Capt	No, but the ship smells very nice now.

Dark   Stop! Put those cans down. I will blast you into space!

Capt   OK, Dark! Cool it! Keep your helmet on!

Prin   Leave them alone, Vaper. It's me you want.

Dark   Ah! The lovely Princess Loofa. I have you at last.

U-B   Meep! meep!

Dark   What did he say?

Prin   He said 'meep meep'.

Dark   What does 'meep meep' mean?

Capt   We don't know. He just says it.

Spick   He always says 'meep meep', don't you, U Bend?

U-B   Meep meep.

Dark   Now, Princess, give me what you took from me.

Prin   Get lost, Vaper. I took nothing!

Dark   You took the secret plans for the Umpire's Death Dump.

12

Capt   A Death Dump! Yuk! That sounds nasty!

Prin   You know what you can do with your secret plans. You get nothing from me.

Dark   We shall see, Princess. We have ways to make you talk.

Capt   Have you got ways to make U-Bend talk as well? We're getting sick of his 'meep meep'.

Dark   Shut up, fool! Now, Princess, how did you get here?

Prin   In a space trash-bin.

Dark   Where is it?

Spick   The trash-bin is in the cargo bay, Lord Vaper.

Dark   My troops will check the trash-bin. Then they will rip this ship to bits to find the plans.

Spick   There were no plans in the bin. There are no plans on this ship.

Prin   You won't find the plans, Vaper. You won't find them because I've got them in my head.

Dark   In your head?

Capt   That's the big round thing on the end of her neck.

Dark   I think I will take you with me, Princess. I will take you to the Umpire.

Spick   No! Not the evil Umpire!

Dark   Yes, the evil Umpire! He will know what to do with your head, Princess.

Capt   Do you mean he's going to give her a hair-cut?

Dark   No! I mean that he will know how to get the plans out of her head.

3-0   Leave the Princess alone.

Prin   Yes, leave me alone. Get away from me, Vaper!

Spick   Tell him, Princess. We're right behind you.

Capt   Yes, about ten miles behind you.

3-0   Leave the Princess and leave this ship.

Dark   Very good. You have a brave robot, Captain. Is he strong? Can he fly? Can he fight?

Capt   No, but he's very good at dusting.

14

Dark   I think I will take him with me. I will take the Princess AND the robot.

Capt   Oh no, please, no, no, no, please don't...

Dark   Stop! I will take the Princess if I want!

Capt   I'm not talking about the Princess. No, no, please don't take the robot!

Prin   Thanks a bunch, Birk.

Spick   Sweepy is our very own robot. We put him together. We made him. He is our friend.

Capt   And don't forget the dusting, Spick. Who is going to do the dusting if Sweepy goes?

Dark   All troops will now beam back to my gun-ship.

3-0   Stay close to me, Princess. I will look after you.

Prin   I'll stick with you, Sweepy. OK, Vaper, let's get on with it.

Dark   Come with me, Princess. The Umpire is waiting.

Capt   Goodbye, Dark. It's been nice to meet you. Don't come again.

Dark   Goodbye, Captain. This time I will let you live.
            But next time…

FX   ZONK ZONK ZONK ZONK.

Narr   So the evil Dark Vaper beamed back. He took
            the Princess and Sweepy 3-0. His gun-ship
            turned away from the Boobyprise. Then it blasted
            off towards the stars.

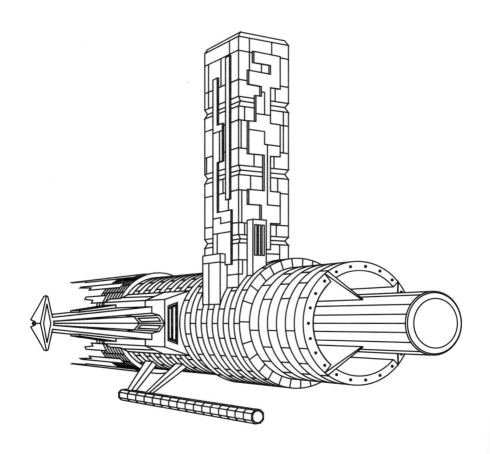

Scene 3: *The Planet Skumm*

Capt   Put the kettle on, Spick.

Spick   We need to move fast, Captain.

Capt   Put the kettle on fast, then.

Spick   We have to find Vaper. We have to rescue the Princess and Sweepy.

Capt   Are you nuts, Spick? How can we do that? Hey, Vaper, give me the Princess or I'll blast you to bits with my bin-lid?

Spick   We must find the Princess and destroy the Death Dump.

Capt   Oh, help! My life used to be just a load of rubbish. Now it's full of Loofas and Death Dumps.

Spick   We can do it, Captain. We can find Vaper and rescue them.

U-B   Meep meep.

Capt   It's OK for you to say meep meep. If I get hurt I end up in sick-bay. If you get hurt they scoot some oil up your antenna and you're as good as new.

Spick   Vaper will take them to the Umpire at the Death Dump. We must find the Death Dump. Then we can find Vaper.

Capt   Where is the Death Dump?

U-B   Meep meep, meep meep.

Spick   I have an idea.

Capt   Good! We'll put the kettle on.

Spick   I know who can tell us where the Umpire is.

Capt   Who?

Spick   Yabba the Shedd.

Capt   Yabba the Shedd? Are you mad, Spick? Is there something up with your three brains?

U-B   Meep meep meep?

Capt   Yabba the Shedd is a crook! He's a monster! And he smells terrible!

U-B   Meep meep poo!

Spick   We've got to do it, Captain. We must do it for the Princess and Sweepy.

Capt   OK, then. I must be nuts! I'll get to the controls.

Spick   Full speed ahead, Captain.

U-B   Meep meep.

Narr   The Boobyprise picked up speed and turned for the planet Skumm. One hour later, the crew beamed down. They stood in front of a massive door. It was Yabba the Shedd's cave.

Capt   Hello? Is there anybody at home? It's the milk man!

Spick   Why don't you knock at the door, Captain?

Capt   OK. Knock knock.

Guard   Who's there?

Capt   Stan.

Guard   Stan who?

Capt   Stan back, we're coming in.

Guard   On your space-bike, pal. You don't get in here!

Spick   Let us in. We must talk with Yabba the Shedd.

Capt   We're from the Bin-ship Boobyprise.

Guard   We don't need our bins done today. We get them done on Friday. Come back on Friday.

Capt   We didn't come to empty the bins.

Spick   We must talk with Yabba the Shedd. It's a matter of life and death.

U-B   Meep meep.

Guard   OK, come on in. I'll take you to Yabba. Leave your guns here.

Spick   We have no guns.

Capt   But we've got an air-freshener. It can bring you out in a nasty rash.

Guard   Lord Yabba, these men are from the Bin-ship Boobyprise.

Yabba   The bin-men come on Friday. Tell them to come back on Friday.

Capt   Wow! Yabba the Shedd! What a smell. I'm glad I've got the air-freshener!

Yabba   Are you a human? I like humans.

Capt   Oh, good. I love you too, Yabba.

Yabba   Yes, I like humans. But I can't eat a whole one!

Spick   My Lord Yabba, we have come for your help. It's a matter of life and death.

Yabba   Tell me.

Spick   Dark Vaper has taken the Princess Loofa. He has taken her to the Umpire at his Death Dump.

Capt   Do you know where it is, Yabb?

Yabba   I can tell you. But you must pay. Can you pay?

Capt   I'm a bit short at the moment, Yabb.

Yabba   Yes, you are short. I like tall humans. They last longer!

Capt   No, Yabba, I'm a bit short of cash. But I can give you the robot.

U-B   MEEEEEEEEEEEP!!

Yabba   I don't like robots. The bits get stuck in my teeth.

Spick   What can we do? How can we pay you?

21

Yabba   You can play with Spot. He's my little pet. We can have some fun. I like that.

Guard   I'll get Spot. He hasn't been fed yet.

Capt   You've got a nice place here, Yabb. That's a nice colour on the walls. What is it?

Yabba   Slime Green.

Spick   Captain, tell me. What is four metres tall, yellow with big claws and long teeth?

Capt   I don't know, Spick. What is it?

Spick   I think it's Spot, and he's behind you.

Capt   Wow! Aagh! Down boy, down boy! Go and fetch the stick!

Yabba   Now for my fun.

Spot   YAAAAARGH! YAAAAARGH!

Spick   Run! Run for the door!

Capt   Wait for me!

U-B   Meep! Meep!

Spot	YAAAARGH! YAAAARGH! YAAAARGH!
Yabba	Guards! Stop them!
Guard	Drop the door! Drop the door!
Capt	He's shutting the door. What shall we do?
U-B	Meep meep! BANG!
Capt	What's U-Bend doing, Spick?
Spick	Look, Captain. U-Bend has got a ray-gun.
U-B	Meep meep! BANG!
FX	POW CRASH
Spick	He's blasted a hole in the door!
Capt	Go for it. Get out!
U-B	Meep meep.
Capt	OK, Spick, beam us up fast. Goodbye, Spot.
Spot	YMMAMARGH!!
FX	ZONK ZONK.

Narr   And back on the Boobyprise the crew went into action.

Capt   OK, Spick, full speed ahead. Get us out of here.

Spick   Full speed ahead, Captain. Wimp speed 10.

Capt   Thanks for getting us out, U-Bend. You're cool.

U-B   Meep meep meep meep.

Capt   Let's have a look at you. You're a clever little robot.

U-B   Meep.

Capt   Where's his ray-gun, Spick?

Spick   There it is, Captain. It pops out like this. There's his video eye. There's his control panel.

Capt   He's got a little satellite dish. And here's a little TV screen. I wonder if he can get SKY TV?

Spick   He's got a screw-driver. And he's got a tin-opener.

Capt   And here's a thing to get stones out of a horse's hoof.

Spick   He must be a Swiss army robot, Captain.

Capt   I wonder why he keeps saying 'meep meep'.

Spick   Look, he's got a little keyboard.

Capt   Yes, it's like a computer.

Spick   Let's try something. Let's tap M-E-E-P out on his keyboard.

Capt   OK.

FX   Tap-tap-tap.

Spick   M-E-E-P

U-B   Meep meep… "Standby. This is the voice of the Umpire. Secret disc XX73. The plans of the Death Dump. On screen now."

Capt   Look, Spick. It's the plans for the Death Dump. U-Bend has got them!

Spick   Yes,Captain. Now we know why he says meep meep. He's been trying to tell us. Now we can rescue the Princess and Sweepy.

Capt   But how can we attack the Death Dump? This is only a bin-ship.

Spick   There is a way, Captain. But we must go back to the beginning.

Capt   I'd like to go back home.

Spick   We must go back to where bin-ships began. Find that wise old bin-man who began it all. He will tell us the way.

Capt   The wise old bin-man!

Spick   Yes, Captain. We must go to Hoova.

Narr   So the Boobyprise set off for Hoova. He was the oldest bin-man of all. A wise old man. Who lived at home alone on the planet Dumestis.

Scene 4: *The Death Dump*

Narr   One side of Dumestis was always day. One side was always night. On the day side there was a swamp. In the swamp there was a tree. Under the tree they found Hoova.

Capt   Is that Hoova?

Spick   I think he's by that rock, Captain.

Capt   No, he's gone now.

Spick   Is he by the tree?

Hoova   Help you can I?

Capt   Hoova! How are you? The dust be with you.

Hoova   The dust be with you, my friend.

Capt   I am Captain Birk. I'm from the Bin-ship Boobyprise.

Hoova   I know you, Birk. Long ago we met.

Capt   This is Spick. This is the robot U-Bend.

U-B   Meep mip moop.

Hoova   We must talk of the stars. We must talk of the planets. But first I'll put the kettle on.

Capt   You are a wise man, Hoova. Can you help us?

Spick   Dark Vaper has taken the Princess Loofa. We must rescue her.

Hoova   Vaper! Evil he is!

Capt   He's taken her to the Umpire. They've gone to the Death Dump.

Hoova   Attack you must. Rescue the Princess.

Spick   But how can we attack the Death Dump?

Capt   It's only a bin-ship. How can we attack with a bin-ship?

Hoova   The Umpire has made a Death Dump. Take him some trash. Dump it.

Spick   That's a good idea!

Capt   Yes, that's a good idea! What is it?

Spick   We dump trash, Captain. We dump it on the Umpire. We dump it on Vaper.

Capt   I like it! Then we can beam down and get the Princess and Sweepy.

U-B   Meep moop mip.

Spick   We need more bin-ships. We need a load of trash.

Capt   No problem. When you want trash just call the Council. We can get the Bin Fleet.

Spick   Yes, the Bin Fleet will help us.

Capt   There's Muck Rogers, and Flush Gordon.

Spick   And we can get Luke Skyscraper, and Dustpan Solo.

Capt   Wow! What a plan. Let's go!

Spick   Thank you, Hoova.

Hoova   Go, my friends. May the dust be with you.

Capt   The dust be with you.

U-B   Meep meep.

Capt   Beam us up, Spick.

FX   ZONK ZONK ZONK.

Narr   The Bin Fleet was on red alert. Five bin-ships met in space. Captain Birk, Muck Rogers, Flush Gordon, Luke Skyscraper and Dustpan Solo. All of them full of trash.

Capt   OK, listen to me. The Umpire is trying to take over.

Spick   He's been taking scrap from space.

Capt   We're going to attack his Death Dump.

Muck   What about Vaper?

Capt   We'll fly in fast.

Spick   Dump your trash on the control room.

Flush   The Umpire will not know what hit him.

Luke   What a mess!

Capt   Then I'll beam down to get Princess Loofa and Sweepy.

Spick   I'll go with you, Captain.

U-B   Meep mip moop.

Solo   May the dust be with you.

Capt   May the dust be with all of us. Let's go. Wimp speed 10.

Narr   So the bin-ships blasted off. Silver streaks in black space. Soon they could see the Death Dump. It was massive.

Capt   There it is, boys.

Muck   Wow!

Flush   Wow!

Luke   Wow!

Solo   Wow!

U-B   Meep!

Muck   Let's go in together. Attack! Attack!

Flush   I'm with you, Muck!

Luke   I can see the control room. Let's dump on it!

Solo   Wait for me!

Narr	The bin-ships swooped down. Trash smashed into the Death Dump. They swooped again. The Captain, Spick and U-Bend beamed down.
Spick	Find the Princess, U-Bend.
U-B	Meep meep.
Spick	This way, Captain.
Capt	Look out for Vaper's troops.
U-B	Mip mip mip.
Spick	Here's the Princess and Sweepy. In here.
Prin	Captain! Spick! Get us out!
Spick	Stand back, Princess. We'll blast the door.
Capt	OK, U-Bend. Blast it!
U-B	Meep meep! BANG!
FX	POW CRASH.
Capt	Come on! Let's go!
3-0	Here we come.

Prin   Wait for me.

Dark   Not so fast, Captain.

Prin   Vaper!

Dark   Get back!

Spick   What shall we do, Captain?

Capt   Quick, Spick! Wiggle your ears!

Spick   OK, Captain. (wiggle wiggle wiggle.)

Dark   Aaargh! Stop it! It's horrible! I can't take it!

Capt   OK, Spick, beam us up fast. Let's get away.

FX   ZONK ZONK ZONK ZONK ZONK.

Narr   But Dark Vaper was not far behind. Spick hit full
            speed on the bin-ship. But as they blasted off,
            the Captain gasped.

Capt   Gasp!

Prin   What's up, Birk?

Capt   It's Vaper. He's after us.

Spick   Red alert! Red alert!

FX   WOOP-WOOP-WOOP-WOOP

U-B   Moop moop moop.

3-0   He's very fast.

Spick   Here he comes, Captain.

Prin   He's firing at us!

FX   POW POW POW.

Dark   This is Dark Vaper. Stop now or I'll blast you.

3-0   We can't get away.

Prin   We can't fight him.

Spick   What are we going to do, Captain?

Capt   I've got an idea!

Prin   Well, hurry up. Vaper's right behind us.

Capt   OK, Spick. I want full speed. Give it all you've got.

Spick   OK, Captain. I'll try to get more speed.

3-0   Oh, hurry, hurry. Vaper is right on our tail!

Capt   That's just where I want him. Are you ready, Spick?

Spick   Yes, Captain.

Capt   Now! Jam the brakes on!

Spick   Brakes on, Captain !

FX   SCRREEEEEEECH!!!

Dark   Aagh! Look out! Don't stop! I'm going to crash!

FX   BANG SMASH CRASH.

Capt   OK, Spick. Full speed ahead. Let's get out of here!

Dark   Stop! Look what you've done! You've bent my gun-ship! It's bust! I'll get you for this. Come back!

Capt   Bye, Dark. We'll see you around.

Spick   Well done, Captain.

3-0   We got away.

U-B   Meep meep.

Capt   It was nothing. Let's go home.

Prin   Well done, Captain. You saved us. I won't forget.

Capt   You're a nice girl,Princess. How about you and me getting together?

Prin   No thanks, Birk. Life's too short and so are you.

Narr   So the Boobyprise turned for home. The Princess was safe. The Council of Planets had got the plans for the Death Dump. But the battle against the evil Umpire would go on.

Capt   Put the kettle on, Spick.